Get into Science

MACHINES
WE USE

Jane Lacey and Sernur Isik

W
FRANKLIN WATTS
LONDON·SYDNEY

Franklin Watts
First published in Great Britain in 2021 by The Watts Publishing Group

Credits
Design and project management: Raspberry Books
Art Direction: Sidonie Beresford-Browne
Designer: Kathryn Davies
Consultant: Sally Nankivell-Aston
Illustrations: Sernur Isik

HB ISBN: 978 1 4451 7030 5
PB ISBN: 978 1 4451 7031 2

Printed in Dubai

FSC
www.fsc.org
MIX
Paper from
responsible sources
FSC® C104740

Franklin Watts
An imprint of
Hachette Children's Group
Part of The Watts Publishing Group
Carmelite House
50 Victoria Embankment
London EC4Y 0DZ

An Hachette UK Company
www.hachette.co.uk

www.franklinwatts.co.uk

www.hants.gov.uk/library

Hampshire County Council

Love YOUR LIBRARY

Tel: 0300 555 1387

CONTENTS

ROLLING ALONG

A log and a block of wood are different shapes. The log is a cylinder and the block of wood is a cuboid.

A **log** will **roll** along when you push it, but when you push a block of **wood**, it will only **slide**.

✋ TRY IT OUT!

Find a cardboard roll and a box like these.
Which one is a cylinder like the log? Which one is a cuboid like the block of wood? Make a slope with a book or a piece of cardboard. Try rolling the box and the cardboard roll down the slope. What happens?

A **cylinder** is a good shape for **rolling**. We can use a cylinder to help us get jobs done.

Is it easier to slide or to roll things along?

TRY IT OUT!

Now try pulling it along over a row of felt-tip pens. Does this make it easier to pull along? Why do you think that is?

MACHINES

A machine is something we use to make work easier.

Scissors, a **knife** and **fork**, a **whisk** and a **spade** are all simple machines.

What jobs do they make easier?

What would it be like if you tried to do those jobs without using anything to help you?

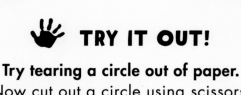

🖐 TRY IT OUT!

Try tearing a circle out of paper.
Now cut out a circle using scissors. What differences do you notice between the two circles?

Could you dig the garden without a spade?

A **washing machine**, a **calculator** and an **iron** are much more **complicated machines**.

Could someone wash clothes, do sums and iron the creases out of clothes without using these machines?

Which one of these machines only needs to be switched on and then does its job by itself?

WHEELS

Wheels are shaped like a circle. They are a good shape for rolling along.

Wheels have to **turn round** on a **rod**.

The **rod** is called an **axle**.

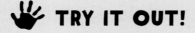

👋 TRY IT OUT!

1. Cut out a circle from thick card and make a hole in the middle of it for the axle.

2. Push a piece of drinking straw through the hole you have made.

3. You can fix the axle to a box like the one in the picture to make a wheelbarrow.

Some of these wheels are for rolling along. Which of these wheels have got other jobs to do?

Look around you when you walk down the street and spot all the things that roll along on wheels.

LOOK AGAIN!

Look again at page 4 to find another shape that is good for rolling. Would a cylinder be a good shape for a wheel?

9

WHEELS with TEETH!

The teeth round the edge of this wheel are called cogs.

A **wheel with cogs** can be used to **turn another wheel with cogs**. When the yellow cog is turned, it makes the other cogs turn round too.

Can you see how the the teeth on the cogs connect to each other?

These machines have wheels with cogs that make them go round and round.

Your **feet push** the bicycle pedals round and round. The **pedals turn** small wheels with cogs round and round. The small wheels turn the bicycle wheels round and round.

Can you see how the small wheels on this bike are linked together?

Do you know which parts of this watch go round and round?

PULLEYS

The suitcase is too heavy to lift easily. A special machine called a pulley can help Ben to lift it.

A **pulley** is made up of a **rope** that runs around **one or more wheels**.

The suitcase is fixed to a pulley wheel with a short rope. Another long rope goes around the first pulley wheel and up and round a second one. Ben is pulling down on the other end of the long rope.

Can he lift the suitcase up now?

The pulley wheels make the job easier.

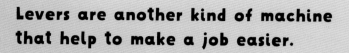

LEVERS

Levers are another kind of machine that help to make a job easier.

The screwdriver and the hammer can be used as levers to lift something up.

When the end of the screwdriver is pushed down it will lift the tin lid up.

What will the hammer lift when it is pulled down?

14

✋ TRY IT OUT!

In order to work, a **lever** must turn around something. The **part it turns** around is called the **fulcrum**.

Find a strong ruler to make a lever, a wooden brick and a book. Try lifting the book on the end of the ruler. What happens?

Now put the brick under the middle of the ruler to make a fulcrum. Try lifting the book with the ruler again.

The book is easier to lift now the ruler is moving around the brick. You are using the ruler as a lever.

15

MORE LEVERS

A wheelbarrow is a different kind of lever that we use to make it easier to lift a heavy load.

The heavy load that needs to be lifted is the pile of leaves.

Can you see that the load is in the middle of the lever?

🔧 LOOK AGAIN!

Look at all the levers on page 15 and 16. Is the load that needs to be lifted in the middle or at one end of each of the levers there?

Oars are **levers** too. When you pull on one end of the oar, the other end pushes through the water and moves the boat along.

A nutcracker, a pair of pliers, a baseball bat and a bottle opener are all levers.

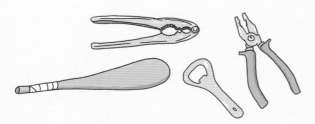

What job does each one do?

What part of the lever do you hold?

Do you pull, push, squeeze or swing the lever to get the job done?

HINGES

Hinges are a special kind of lever. They join two things together but still let them bend and move.

Did you know that hinges join some of the bones in your body together?

Imagine what would happen if your bones were all firmly fixed together and not joined with hinges!

👋 TRY IT OUT!

Bend your knees. Bend your elbows. Open and shut your mouth. Can you feel the hinges in your elbows, your knees and your jaw letting your bones bend and move?

Hinges are used to fasten things together that have to open and shut and fold.

A door opens and shuts on hinges. Try pushing a door open near the hinges. Now try pushing it near the handle. Which is easier?

BALANCING

Jessie and Ben are balancing on the see-saw because they are both about the same weight.

What would happen to the see-saw if Dad was on one end and Ben was on the other?

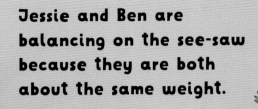

The scales are balanced because both pans of apples weigh the same.

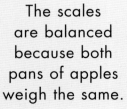

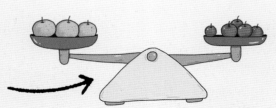

What would happen to the scales if a leaf was in one pan and a stone was in the other?

All kinds of things use balance to help them to work properly.

The flour in the pan is balancing with the weights on the other side of the kitchen scales.

The cook has used a 1 kg weight. How much flour has she put on the scales?

1kg

The elephants on this mobile hang evenly because they have been carefully balanced.

What would happen if this large elephant was swapped with a smaller one on the mobile?

💡 THINK ABOUT IT!

A balance is another type of lever. Where are the fulcrums on the see-saw and the kitchen scales?

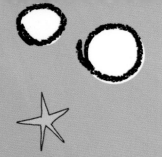

SLOPES
and SCREWS

Harry can push along a heavy load in a wheelbarrow.

He has made a slope with a plank to help him to push the load up the step.

A **slope** is a kind of **simple machine** that makes **lifting a heavy load easier**.

The slope that winds round the screw helps to force it into the wood. When you turn the screw round and round, the wood moves up the slope. This pulls the screw little by little into the wood.

Can you see a slope on this screw? A drill bit has a slope on it too!

✋ TRY IT OUT!

Cut out a paper triangle shape like this one. Now wind the triangle round a pencil. Can you see the spiral shape you have made? It is just like the spiral slope round the screw and drill bit.

MAKING things GO

This metal spring is shaped like a spiral. If you squash it down, it will spring back into shape when you let it go.

✋ TRY IT OUT!

Fold a strip of card backwards and forwards. Tape the end down and squash down the top. Let it go and watch the card spring back up. You can use a spring like this to make a pop-up card.

✋ TRY IT OUT!

Tie each end of a long piece of string around the middle of a long wooden brick. Twist the brick round and round until the string is wound up tightly. Let the brick go and watch it turn round and round as the string unwinds.

How would you make this toy go?

When the key is turned, it winds up a metal coil inside the toy. As the coil unwinds, it moves the toy along.

All machines need something to make them go.

What needs a spring to make it go?

Can you spot something that needs to be switched on?

What needs to be wound up to make it go?

What needs someone to work hard to make it go?

✿ LOOK AGAIN!

Look at all the different machines in the book.
Can you tell what makes each one go?

USEFUL WORDS

FULCRUM
A fulcrum is the fixed point or edge a lever turns round.

HINGE
A hinge joins two things together but still lets them move. Hinges attach a door to its frame, but still let it open and close.

JOB
A job is a special piece of work to be done.

LEVER
A lever is a bar that turns around a fixed point. Levers can help to make a job easier to do.

MACHINE
A machine is something we use to make a job easier.

PULL
People and machines can pull. An engine on a train pulls carriages along. When we pull something, it usually moves towards us.

AXLE
An axle is a rod that goes through the centre of a wheel. A wheel turns round on an axle.

BALANCING
When two objects that weigh the same amount are put on scales, the scales are balancing. If one object is heavier, it will make the scales go down on one side.

COG WHEEL
A cog wheel is a wheel with teeth all round the edge.

PULLEY

A pulley is a machine made of ropes and wheels. It makes it easier to lift heavy loads.

PUSH

People and machines can push. A bulldozer pushes earth out of the way. When we push something, it moves away from us.

SCALES

Scales are machines that measure how much things weigh.

SCREW

A screw is a simple machine. It is a cylinder shape with a slope wound round it.

SLOPE

A slope is like a gentle hill. Slopes can be used as simple machines. It is easier to walk or push things up a gentle slope than up a steep hill.

SPRING

A spring is a piece of wire that has been coiled round and round. When you stretch it or squash it down and then let it go, it springs back into shape again.

SWING

Something that is hanging down, like a swing in a park, will swing backwards and forwards when it is pushed. Some levers swing around their fulcrum.

WEIGHT

You can find out how heavy an object is by measuring its weight. The weight of an object can be measured on weighing scales.

WHEEL

A wheel is a circular shaped machine that helps us do a job. Wheels turn round on axles.

WORK

Work is done when something is moved or stopped. People and machines can both do work.

QUIZ

Now it's time to see how much you have learned. Try out this quick quiz to test your knowledge.

1 Which of these shapes is best for rolling?
a) Cylinder
b) Cuboid
c) Cube

2 What do we call something we use to make work easier?
a) Hat
b) Snack
c) Machine

3 Which of these is an example of a simple machine?
a) Scissors
b) Washing machine
c) Car

4 What is the name of the rod that wheels turn on?
a) Ant
b) Axle
c) Arch

5 What is the name of a wheel with teeth round the edge?
a) Cog
b) Axle
c) Watch

6 Which of these machines can help you lift heavy loads?
a) Washing machine
b) Pulley
c) Iron

7 To work, a lever must turn round a...
a) Screw
b) Cog
c) Fulcrum

8 What parts of your body can be joined by a hinge?
a) Bones
b) Hairs
c) Nails

9 For scales to balance both items need to...
a) Be red
b) Weigh the same
c) Be the same size

10 What shape is a spring?
a) Spiral
b) Cuboid
c) Square

FURTHER INFORMATION

BOOKS TO READ

- *Infographic How It Works: Machines and Motors* by Jon Richards and Ed Simkins (Wayland 2019)
- *Science Makers: Making with Machines* by Anna Claybourne (Wayland, 2020)

WEBSITES TO VISIT

- **Learn more about simple machines and how they work with DK Findout**: Simple Machines: https://www.dkfindout.com/uk/science/simple-machines
- **Use your knowledge of machines to help Twitch in this game from the Museum of Science and Industry in Chicago:** https://www.msichicago.org/play/simplemachines

ATTRACTIONS TO EXPLORE

Visit the **National Museum of Scotland** in Edinburgh to find out about inventions of all kinds. Don't miss the aerial history of aviation above your heads! Head to the **Science and Industry Museum** in Manchester to be inspired by machines from the past, and see how they influenced the gadgets we use today. Explore the **London Transport Museum** to discover vehicles from the past and imagine how we might travel in the future!

NOTE TO PARENTS AND TEACHERS

Every effort has been made by the publisher to ensure that these websites contain no inappropriate or offensive material. However, because of the nature of the Internet, it is impossible to guarantee that the content of these sites will not be altered. We strongly advise that Internet access is supervised by a responsible adult.

ABOUT THIS BOOK

Children are natural scientists. They learn by touching and feeling, noticing, asking questions and trying things out for themselves. The books in the *Get into Science* series are designed for the way children learn. Familiar objects are used as starting points for further learning. *Machines We Use* starts with a rolling log and explores simple machines.

Each double page spread introduces a new topic, such as levers. Information is given, questions asked and activities suggested that encourage children to make discoveries and develop new ideas for themselves. Look out for these panels throughout the book:

TRY IT OUT! indicates a simple activity, using safe materials that proves or explores a point.

THINK ABOUT IT! indicates a question inspired by the information on the page but points the reader to areas not covered by the book.

LOOK AGAIN! introduces a cross-referencing activity that links themes and facts throughout the book.

Encourage children not to take the familiar world for granted. Point things out, ask questions and enjoy making scientific discoveries together.

INDEX

Forces Around Us

- Falling down
- Heavy or light?
- What is a force?
- Standing firm
- Push and pull
- Press
- Squash and stretch
- Stop and start
- Rubbing together
- Drag
- Magnetism

Full of Energy

- Working hard
- Feeling hungry
- Animal energy
- Plant energy
- Full of energy
- Changing energy
- Electricity
- Switch it on
- Keeping warm
- Moving along
- Sun, wind and water

Light and Dark

- Light and dark
- Daylight
- Darkness
- Casting shadows
- Seeing
- Reflection
- Shining through
- Bigger and smaller
- Snapshot
- Rainbows
- A colourful world

Machines We Use

- Rolling along
- Machines
- Wheels
- Wheels with teeth
- Pulleys
- Levers
- More levers
- Hinges
- Balancing
- Slopes and screws
- Making things go

Solid, Liquid or Gas?

- Useful materials
- Pouring
- Gas
- Water
- Water test
- Melting
- Changing shapes
- Dissolving
- Paper
- What material?
- Natural or made?

The Five Senses

- The five senses
- Seeing
- Two eyes
- Hearing
- Listen to this!
- Touch
- Smell
- Paper
- Sniffing out
- Taste
- Keeping safe

Time

- What's the time?
- Time passing
- Day and night
- Measuring time
- Counting the hours
- What's the date?
- A year
- Seasons
- Natural clocks
- Always changing
- Fast and slow

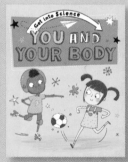

You and Your Body

- Name the parts
- You are special
- Making sense
- Eating and drinking
- Keeping healthy
- Skin
- Under the skin
- Breathing
- Pumping blood
- On the Move
- Sleep well

W
FRANKLIN
WATTS